JavaScript

Interview Questions
You'll Most Likely Be Asked

Second Edition

Job Interview Questions Series

 **Vibrant Publishers**

www.vibrantpublishers.com

JavaScript Interview Questions
You'll Most Likely Be Asked

Second Edition

© 2012, By Vibrant Publishers, USA. All rights reserved. No part of this publication may be reproduced or distributed in any form or by any means, or stored in a database or retrieval system, without the prior permission of the publisher.

ISBN-10:1453870997
ISBN-13: 9781453870990

Library of Congress Control Number: 2010938816

Vibrant Publishers books are available at special quantity discount for sales promotions, or for use in corporate training programs. For more information please write to **bulkorders@vibrantpublishers.com**

Please email feedback / corrections (technical, grammatical or spelling) to **spellerrors@vibrantpublishers.com**

To access the complete catalogue of Vibrant Publishers, visit **www.vibrantpublishers.com**

Table of Contents

This page is intentionally left blank

JavaScript Interview Questions

Review these typical interview questions and think about how you would answer them. Read the answers listed; you will find best possible answers along with strategies and suggestions.

This page is intentionally left blank

Introduction to JavaScript

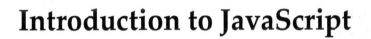

1: What is JavaScript and what does it do?

Answer:

JavaScript is a scripting language that adds interactivity to HTML pages.

2: What kind of language does JavaScript provide?

Answer:

JavaScript is an interpreted language that executes scripts without preliminary compilation.

3: Is there any connection between Java and JavaScript?

Answer:

No. They are different in every way and JavaScript is not as powerful and complex as Java.

4: What is the official name of JavaScript and is it supported by all browsers?

Answer:

The official name of JavaScript is ECMA (European Computer Manufacturer's Association) and with it, Internet Explorer 4 and Mozilla Firefox 1.5 fully supported.

5: What does JavaScript do?

Answer:

JavaScript is meant to be an easy scripting language that helps the non-programmers with its simple syntax. JavaScript is smart enough that it can put dynamic text into HTML pages, it can react to events (like when a page has finished downloading), and it can read and write HTML elements, create cookies and so forth.

6: Does prior knowledge of JAVA ease the use of JavaScript?

Answer:

Yes. Being modeled after Java, which in turn is modeled after C++, JavaScript should be easier to familiarize and work with.

7: Is JavaScript case sensitive?

Answer:
Yes. Unlike HTML, JavaScript has to have all variables and function names (etc.) in capital letters.

8: How do you place JavaScript?
Answer:
JavaScript may be inserted into code with the following syntax:
<script type="text/JavaScript">

9: Where do you place JavaScript?
Answer:
JavaScript may be placed in the <head> or <body> section of HTML code, but it is usually a good practice to place it in the <head> as to not hinder your code later on.

This page is intentionally left blank

Statements, Comments and Variables

10: How do you terminate statements in JavaScript?
Answer:
In JavaScript, statements are terminated by semicolons (;) and although they are not mandatory they are a good practice to pick up.

11: Why are comments used in JavaScript and how are they inserted?
Answer:
Usually comments are added to make the code more readable but they can also be used to explain the code. They are inserted with // (for single line comments) and /* */ for multiple lines comments.

12: What are variables and how are they inserted?
Answer:
Variables are storing containers used for holding expressions and values. They can have a short letter or a longer name and are inserted with the statement: var. Because the variables are loosely typed, they can hold any type of data.

13: What does a variable of var y=10; and var catname= "Tomcat"; do?
Answer:
With the execution of the above code, we have variables that hold values of 10(for y) and Tomcat (for catname).
Note that the inclusion of text warrants " " being used.

14: How many statements types can we find in JavaScript? Give some examples?
Answer:
The statement types found in JavaScript are: Expression statements, compound, empty and labeled statements.
Example: break, continue, default, do, for, etc.

15: What are conditional statements and how are they implemented in JavaScript?

Answer:
Conditional statements are used to perform and act on different sets of conditions declared by the programmer. They are the following: if statement; if...else statement; if...else if...else statement and the switch statement.

16: How will you determine a variable type in JavaScript?
Answer:
A variable type in JavaScript is determined using Typeof operator. When the object is String, Number, Function, undefined and Boolean, the operator returns the same type. And when the object is null and array, the operator returns "object".
Example:
var count=100;
typeof count; ⟶ (returns "number")

17: What is the difference in evaluating ["8"+5+2] and [8+5+"2"]?
Answer:
In ["8"+5+2],"8" is a String. So anything that trail the string will be changed to string. Hence the result will be"852".
In [8+5+"2"], 8 and 5 are integer, so it gets added up (13).And "2" is treated as String. Hence the concatenation takes place and the result will be "132".

18: Is it possible to assign a string to a floating point variable?
Answer:
Yes. Any variable can be assigned to another data type. For example,
var a1=10.39;
document.write(a1); ⟶ 10.39
a1="hai";
document.write(a1); ⟶ hai

19: Will variable redeclaration affect the value of that variable?
Answer:
No. The same value will be retained in the variable.

Example:
```
var status="cool";
document.write("status"); //cool
var status;
document.write("status"); //cool
status="chill";
document.write("status"); //chill
```

20: How will you search a matching pattern globally in a string?
Answer:
A matching pattern can be globally searched in a string using "g" modifier in Regular Expression.
Example:
```
var p1="First_Regular_ Expression_First";
var q1="/First/g";
document.write("Pattern_Match:" + p1.match(q1)); //
Pattern_Match:First,First
```

21: How will you search a particular pattern in a string?
Answer:
A particular pattern in string can be searched using test function. If the match is found it returns true, else false.
Example:
```
var my_pattern1=new RegExp("pp");
document.write(my_pattern1.test("Happy_Days")); //true
```

22: Which property is used to match the pattern at the start of the string?
Answer:
"^" symbol is used for position matching.
Example:
```
var p1="First_Regular_ Expression_First";
var q1="/First/^";
document.write("Pattern_Match:" + p1.match(q1));
//Pattern_Match:First ⟶ First_Regular
```

23: Which property is used to match the pattern at the end of the string?

Answer:

"$" symbol is used for end position matching.

Example:

var p1="First_Regular_ Expression_First";

var q1="/First/$";

document.write("Pattern_Match:" + p1.match(q1));

//Pattern_Match:First ⟶ Expression_First

This page is intentionally left blank

Operators and Functions

24: What are operators? Which are the most important operators in JavaScript?

Answer:

Operators in JavaScript are used to combine values that form expressions. The most important are: = and +. The first is used to assign values and the second one is used to add values together.

25: Why comparison and logical operators are used?

Answer:

Comparison operators are used to determine if there is a difference between variables, and also their equality, while the logical operators are used to determine the logic of variables.

26: How many types of pop-up boxes does JavaScript have? What are those?

Answer:

JavaScript has three types of pop-up boxes and they are: alert, confirm and prompt.

27: Does creating an alert box prompt the user to respond with OK or Cancel?

Answer:

No. An alert box only gives the user the option of choosing OK to proceed.

28: What are functions in JavaScript and where are they placed?

Answer:

Functions contain code that is executed before an event thus stopping the browser from loading a script when the page opens. Functions can be placed both in the <head> or <body> section, but it is advised to place them in the <head> section.

Values, Arrays and Operators

29: What does the keyword null mean in JavaScript?
Answer:
The keyword null is a special value that indicates no value. It is unique from other values and also fully distinct.

30: What does the value undefined mean in JavaScript?
Answer:
Undefined is a special value in JavaScript, it means the variable used in the code does not exist or is not assigned any value or the property does not exist.

31: Do the null and undefined values have the same conversion in Boolean, numeric and string context?
Answer:
No. The undefined value changes into Nan in numeric context and undefined in a string context. They share the same conversion in Boolean.

32: What are Boolean values?
Answer:
Boolean values are datatypes that only have two types of values: true or false; a value of Boolean type only represents the truth: it says if it true or not.

33: Can a Boolean value be converted into numeric context?
Answer:
Yes. If it is converted into numeric context the true value becomes 1 and if it is a false value it becomes a 0.

34: What happens when a number is dropped where a Boolean value is expected to be?
Answer:
The number is converted into a true value, but only if it not equal to 0 or NaN which in turn is converted into a false value.

35: What are objects in JavaScript?

Answer:
Objects are collections of named values that most of the times are referred to as properties of an object.

36: What is an array in JavaScript?

Answer:
An array is a collection of data values which can handle more than one value at a time, the difference being that each data in an array has a number or index.

37: From which version forward has JavaScript stopped using ASCII character set?

Answer:
From v.3 JavaScript started using Unicode character sets: identifiers can now contain letters and digits from the Unicode complete character set.

38: What is the scope of a variable in JavaScript?

Answer:
The scope of a variable is the region in which your program in which it is defined. Thus a global variable has a global scope meaning it is defined everywhere in your JavaScript code. The local variables have a local scope meaning they are defined only in the body section of your code.

39: In the body of the code which variable with the same name has more importance over the other: the local or the global variable?

Answer:
In the body of a function a local variable will always take precedence over a global variable hiding it all together.

40: How many types of undefined variables can we find in JavaScript?

Answer:
There are two kinds of undefined variables: the first is the one that

has never been declared and the second is the kind of undefined variable that has been declared but has never had a value assigned to it.

41: What are the (==) (===) and what do they do in JavaScript?
Answer:
The first (==) is the equality operator and it checks if its two operands are equal. The second (===) is called the identity operator and it checks if two operands are identical by using a strict definition.

42: How many types of operators can we find in JavaScript?
Answer:
There are eight types of operators in JavaScript. These are as follows: operator, arithmetic, equality, relational, string, logical, bitwise and miscellaneous.

43: How many types of comparison operators does JavaScript contain?
Answer:
There are four types of comparison operators in JavaScript. They are: less than (<); greater than (>); less than or equal (<=) and greater than or equal (>=).

44: Can comparison be done on any type of operands?
Answer:
Yes. Operands in JavaScript that are not number or strings are converted.

45: What are logical operators and how are they used in JavaScript?
Answer:
The logical operators perform Boolean algebra and are used mostly with comparison operators to show complex comparisons that involve more than one variable.

46: Does JavaScript contain classes?
Answer:
Yes. Although they do not define the structure of an object like in Java and C++, it does approximate the classes with its constructors and their prototype objects.

47: What is an object in JavaScript?
Answer:
An object is an instance of its class. This allows us to have multiple instances of any class.

48: How are classes and objects in JavaScript named and why?
Answer:
Classes are named with an initial capital letter and an object with lowercase letters. This ensures that classes and objects are distinct from each other.

49: What are class properties in JavaScript?
Answer:
Class property is associated with a class itself and not instance of a class. This ensures that no matter how many instances of a class are created only one copy of each class property exists.

50: What are class methods in JavaScript?
Answer:
Class methods are associated with a class rather than an instance of a class, meaning they are invoked by the class itself and not an instance of the class.

51: Do class properties and class methods have a global and local range?
Answer:
No. They are both only global because they do not operate on a particular object.

52: How do JavaScript equality operators compare objects?

Answer:
Equality operators compare objects by reference and not by value, checking to see if both references are to the same object. They do not check to see if two objects have the same property names and values.

53: Are the null and undefined values for the variable same?
Answer:
No. Variables that are declared and not assigned any value will have undefined values whereas the variable that is assigned a null will have null values.
Example:
var qno; ⟶ "undefined value"
var Items=10;
Items=null; ⟶ "null value"

54: What is the difference between "===" and "=="?
Answer:
   a) "===" returns true - if both the operands are same and has same data type
   b) "==" checks only for operands - if both are same, returns true

For comparison of operands, JavaScript converts different data type to same type.
Example:
Let p=3
p=='3' //true   p=='3' //false
3=='3' //true   3=='3' //false
P==3 //true   P==3 //true

55: What is the function of delete operator in JavaScript?
Answer:
It deletes
   a) an object
      Syntax: delete obj_name1;

b) particular element in an array
   Syntax: delete arr_ele1[index];
c) property of an object
   Syntax: delete obj_name2.prop_name;

56: How will you clip the particular portion of an element?
Answer:
Using clip property of the style object, we can clip a particular portion of an element.
Example:
my_obj1.style.clip="values";
my_obj1 $\longrightarrow$ document object, getElementById property
values $\longrightarrow$ auto(Unclip),rect(top1,right1,botttom1,left1)-pin the shape defined by value.

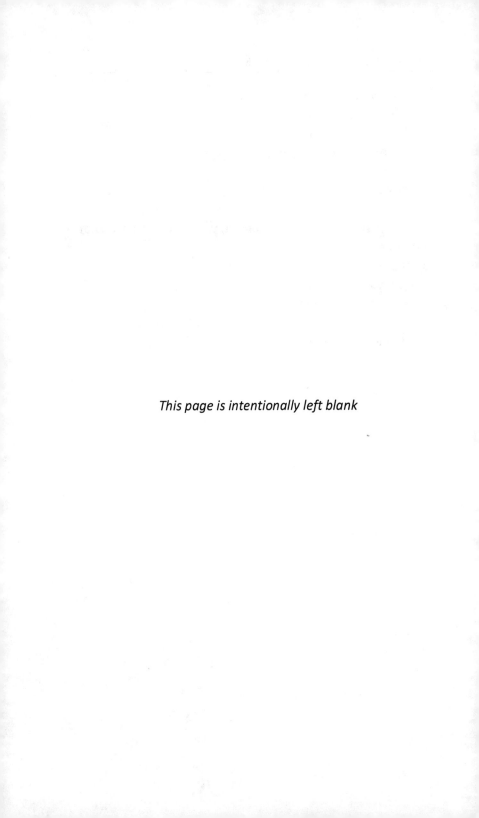

This page is intentionally left blank

Modules, Characters and Attributes

57: How is a module in JavaScript written so that it can be used by any script or module?

Answer:
The most important rule is to never define global variables as to have the risk of having that value overwritten by a module or another programmer.

58: How are regular expressions represented and created in JavaScript?

Answer:
Regular expressions are represented by the RegExp objects and are created by the RegExp() constructor or a special literal syntax.

59: How do you combine literal characters in JavaScript?

Answer:
Literal characters can be combined into character classes by placing them within square brackets.

60: What document properties does a document contain?

Answer:
In a document we can find the following properties: bgcolor, cookie, domain, lastModified, location, referrer, title and URL.

61: How many types of DOM document object collections can we find in JavaScript?

Answer:
There are five DOM properties that give access to special elements within a document: anchors, applets, forms, images and links.

62: Does use of DOM properties allow you to change the structure of a document?

Answer:
No. Using these properties you can inspect and alter a link and read values from a link but the text in the document cannot be changed; the structure of the document cannot be altered.

63: How are document objects named in JavaScript?

Answer:

Documents are named with the name attribute of forms. You can change elements, links and images when the name attribute is present. Its value is used for exposure to the corresponding object by name.

This page is intentionally left blank

Event Handlers and DOM

64: How are event handlers defined in JavaScript?
Answer:
Event handlers are defined by assigning a function to an event handler property, unlike HTML where event handlers are defined by giving a string of JavaScript code to an event handler attribute.

65: What do the HTMLInputElement and HTMLFormElementinterfaces define in HTML DOM?
Answer:
The HTMLInputElement defines focus() and blur() methods and form property. HTMLFormElementinterfaces defines submit() and reset() methods and length property.

66: How many levels of DOM standard are currently released?
Answer:
There are two levels of DOM: the first one was released in 1998 and it defines the core DOM interfaces. The second level that was released in 2000 that updates the core interfaces and defines standard APIs for working with document events style sheets CSS.

67: Are there any more levels of DOM?
Answer:
Yes there are. One of them is the level 3 DOM, but its features are not fully supported by all the web browsers and the other is the level0 DOM whish in fact is the legacy DOM.

68: What does the Node interface define in DOM?
Answer:
The node interface defines the childNotes, firstChild, lastChild, nextSibling and previousSibling properties.

69: How do you find document elements in a HTML document?
Answer:
You can find elements by using the getElementsByTagName and obtain any type of HTML element.

70: How are documents created and modified in DOM?

Answer:
Documents are modified by setting attribute values on document elements with the element.setAttribute() method. They are created with document.createDocumentFragment().

71: How can you build a DOM tree of arbitrary document content?

Answer:
You can achieve this by creating new Element and text nodes with the Document.CreateElement() and Document.CreateTextNote() methods; you can then add them to a document with the Note.AppendChild(), Note.InsertBefore() and Note.replaceChild() methods.

72: How do you find document elements in IE4?

Answer:
Because IE4 does not support the getElementById() and get ElementsBytagName()methods we are forced to use the array property named all().

73: How to access Html attributes using DOM?

Answer:
Using three methods of DOM:
   a) **getAttribute():** Retrives the value of an attribute
   b) **setAttribute():** Modifies the value of an attribute
   c) **removeAttribute():** Removes the entire attributes from an element

74: What is the difference between getAttribute() and getAttributeNode()?

Answer:
   a) **getAttribute():** returns the value of an attribute
   b) **getAttributeNode():** returns the attribute itself

Example:

```
<body>
<p id="ki" attr="Ish">Hellllo</p>
    <script>
        txt1=document.getElementById('ki').getAttribute('attr');
        document.write(txt1 + "<br>");
        txt2=document.getElementById('ki').getAttributeNode('att
        r');
        document.write(txt2.name +"  :   ");
        document.write(txt2.value);
    </script>
</body>
```

75: What are the event handlers in JavaScript?
Answer:
Event handlers are the JavaScript code that can be used inside the Html tags and gets executed when any events such as form submission, page loading occur. Some of the event handlers in JavaScript are:
   a) onload
   b) onunload
   c) onclick
   d) onmouseout
   e) onmouseover

76: Can you use two or more functions in onclick event?
Answer:
By separating the functions with semicolon(;) we can use two or more functions. First function gets executed after onclick event. The consecutive functions get executed only when the immediate previous function returns true.
Example:
onclick=("my_fun1();my_fun2();my_fun3()");

Keywords, CSS and CSS2

77: What is the "this" keyword in JavaScript?
Answer:
When an event handler with an HTML or JavaScript property is defined a function to a property of a document element is assigned. When the event handler is invoked the "this" keyword refers to the target element.

78: What does lexically scoped in JavaScript mean?
Answer:
It means that functions run in the scope that they are defined in and not in the scope they are called in.

79: Is the following expression correct: element.style.font-family= "arial";?
Answer:
No. It is incorrect because in JavaScript many CSS style attributes contain hyphens in their names and these are interpreted as minus signs.

Statements and Functions

80: How can you replace an if-else statement in JavaScript?

Answer:

You can simply replace if-else statement by using the ternary operator. These kinds of operators require three operands. The ternary operator can be defined as follows:

(condition) ? val1 :val2.

81: What is a "memoization" method in JavaScript?

Answer:

Memoization is an optimization technique used in JavaScript. Functions may use objects to remember the results of previous operations, in this way avoiding unnecessary work.

82: What does 2+3+"1" evaluate to?

Answer:

As 2 and 3 are integers, 2+3 will evaluate to 5. Since "1" is a string, it will concatenate with 5 and the final result will be the string "51"

Roles of JavaScript, Scripts and Events

83: Give some examples of the role that JavaScript has on the Web.

Answer:

The role of JavaScript is to provide a better user browsing experience. JavaScript can do many things like: creating visual effects such as image rollovers, sorting the columns of a table, so the user can easily find what he needs and hiding certain content.

84: Give an example on how JavaScript can be used in URLs.

Answer:

JavaScript can be used in URLs, using "JavaScript:" pseudoprotocol specifier. This specifies that the body of the URL is an arbitrary string of JavaScript code to be run by the JavaScript interpreter. It is treated as a single line of code, and the statements must be separated by semicolons. A JavaScript URL can look like this one:

JavaScript:varJavaScript:varJavaScript:varJavaScript:varJavaScript:varJavaScript:varJavaScript:varJavaScript:varJavaScript:varJavaScript:varJavaSc ript:varJavaScript:varJavaScript:varJavaScript:varJavaScript:varJavaScript:varJavaScript:var today = new Date(); "<p>The date is:</p>" + today;

85: How are scripts in JavaScript executed?

Answer:

Scripts are executed in the order in which they appear and the code in the <script> tags is executed as part of document loading process.

86: What do scripts placed in the <head> part of an HTML document do?

Answer:

Scripts placed in the <head> section usually define functions that are to be called by other code and/or declare and initialize variables used by other code.

87: What do scripts placed in the <body> part of an HTML

document do?

Answer:

Scripts placed in the <body> part of a document can do everything that those placed in a <head> section of the document do. They can also manipulate document elements that appear before the script.

88: When does the browser fire an onload event?

Answer:

The browser fires an onload event and runs any JavaScript code that has been registered after the document has been parsed, all scripts have run and all auxiliary content has finished loading. In short, for all major browsers (except IE), the JavaScript onload event doesn't fire when the page loads as a result of a Back button operation - it only fires when the page is first loaded.

89: When does the onunload event trigger and what does it do?

Answer:

The onunload event triggers after the user navigates away from the web page giving the code on that page a final chance to run; the onunload event enables the possibility to undo effects of your onload handler or scripts in the web page.

90: What about reading, writing a file? How can we do this in JavaScript?

Answer:

Client-side JavaScript does not provide any way to read, write or delete files or directories on the client computer. This is also a security aspect – with no File object and no file access functions a JavaScript program cannot delete a user's data.

91: What is "cross-site scripting"?

Answer:

Cross Site Scripting (XSS) is the name of a security issue in which an attacker injects HTML tags or scripts into a website. Even though defending this kind of attacks is a job for server-side developers, JavaScript programmers must also be aware of, and defend against cross-site scripting.

92: What are JavaScript timers? Give examples and explain one of them.

Answer:

It is very important for any programming environment to have the ability to schedule code to be executed at some point in the future. Client-side JavaScript provides some global functions like: setTimeout(), clearTimeout(), setInterval(), clearInterval(). For example setTimeout() method schedules a function to run after a specific number of milliseconds elapses.

93: What is the "History" object?

Answer:

The history property of the Window object refers to the History object for the window. The History object supports three methods: back(), forward() and go(). The first 2 methods are similar with what happens when the user clicks on the Back and Forward browser buttons. The go() method takes an integer argument and can skip any number of pages

94: What is the "Screen" object?

Answer:

The screen property of the Window object refers to a Screen object that provides information about the size of the user's display, the number of colors available on it. The "width" and "height" properties can be used to specify the size of the display in pixels.

95: What is the "Navigator" object?

Answer:

The navigator property of a Window object refers to a Navigator object that contains important information about the web browser, such as the version and the list of data formats it can display. In the past Navigator object was used by scripts to determine if they were running in Internet Explorer or in Netscape web browser.

96: What is "onreset" in JavaScript?

Answer:

Onreset is an event handler of a form object in JavaScript. It gets executed when the reset button in the form is clicked and resets the fields when it receives true value otherwise prevent the form elements from being reset.

Example:

onreset="alert('AABBCC')"

97: What is void 0 in JavaScript?

Answer:

a) JavaScript files can be executed directly in the web browsers by placing "JavaScript:" before the code

b) Web browsers attempt to load the page when any value returning JavaScript's code is executed

c) void 0 is used to prevent the unwanted action

98: What is the best practice to place the JavaScript codes?

Answer:

Place all JavaScript codes in one place. So it can be placed,

a) At the end of html tag

b) Below second header tag

c) Before the closing of bod tag

99: How to prevent caching of web pages in temporary internet files folder?

Answer:

By adding <META HTTP-EQUIP="PRAGMA" CONTENT="NO-CACHE" > in the second header tag which is placed before the html's end tag(</html>).

Example:

```
<html>
    < head >
        <META HTTP-EQUIV="REFRESH" CONTENT="3">
    </ head >
```

```
<body>
    <p>Helllo</p>
</body>
< head >
    <META Http-equiv="PRAGMA" Content="NO-CACHE">
</head>
</ html >
```

100: Why adding of meta tag in first header will not prevent caching of the Web page?
Answer:
The browsing page gets cached only when the buffer is half filled. So when the meta tag is added in first header, the internet explorer search for that page in cache at that instant. Most of the time, buffer won't get half filled at the beginning of parsing.

101: What is the purpose of meta tag?
Answer:
When this tag is read while parsing the html code, internet explorer searches for this page in cache at that instant. If it is found, it will be removed from the cache.
Syntax:
```
<META Http-equiv="PRAGMA" Content="NO-CACHE">
```

102: How will you resolve looping problem in JavaScript?
Answer:
Using closures which combines the function with its referencing environment, looping can be resolved. It keeps the local variable of the function alive even after the function returned the value. When there is function within the function, Closure is created.

103: Give any example for resolving looping problem.
Answer:
```
var method1={};
for(var k=0;k<5;k++){
    method1[i]=function(){
```

```
        document.write("Iteration:" + k + "< >");
    };
}
for(var m=0;m<5;m++){
        method1[j]();
}
```

Output:
4 4 4 4 4 instead of 0 1 2 3 4

By adding closure,this can be rectified.

```
method1[i]=function(n){
    return function(){
        document.write("Iteration:" + n + "< >");
    }
})(k);
```

Output:
0 1 2 3 4

104: When is the Execution context created and what are the primary components?
Answer:
During execution of JavaScript function, the execution context is created. It keeps track of the execution of its related code. Global execution context is created when executing the application.

  a) **LexicalEnvironment:** Resolves the identifier references
  b) **VariableEnvironment:** Records the variable-function declaration bindings
  c) **ThisBinding:** value of "this" keyword related with execution context

105: When is the Execution context stack created?
Answer:
  a) **Global execution context:** Created when executing the application

b) **New execution context:** Created when the new functions are created

c) **Collection of this execution context form the execution context stack**

106: How is the outer scope environment references maintained?

Answer:

Using LexicalEnvironment, the outer scope environment references are maintained. It contains two components:

a) **Environment Record:** Identifier bindings are stored for the execution context

b) **Outer Refernces:** Points to the declaration of execution context in lexicalEnvironment

107: How will you read or write in a file using JavaScript?

Answer:

An I/O operation such as reading or writing is not possible. However, "Java Applet" can be implemented to read files for script.

108: How will you create rich, responsive display and editor user interface?

Answer:

Using knockout we can create rich, responsive display and editor user interface. It is JavaScript library which implements the model view-viewmodel pattern. It is used to create UI and allows dynamic updation and can be used with any server or client.

109: Which is the new JavaScript engine developed for internet explorer9 by Microsoft?

Answer:

Chakra is the new Javascript engine for IE9. A distinct feature is that its JIT compiles scripts on separate "CPUcore", parallel to web browsers. The engine also accesses the computer's graphic processing unit for 3D videos and graphics. To execute scripts on traditional web pages and to improve JavaScript runtime and libraries, a new interpreter was included.

110: What is Node.js?

Answer:

Node.js is a software designed for creating server side JavaScript application which is not executed in client browser. It is event based and runs asynchronously to provide scalability and reduce overhead.

111: Which is alternative to XML for data exchange in JavaScript?

Answer:

JSON (JavaScript Object Notation). Light weighted, text-based data exchange format. Web data is imported into JavaScript applications using JSON.

Example: JSON Object creation

var obj_json1={"Company_name":"ABC","Experiance":"5"};
document.write("Co Name:" + obj_json1.Company_name); //Co Name:ABC

112: What are the sub-components of dynamic component in JavaScript?

Answer:

a) **Dynamic typing:** Based on values; not associated on variable

b) **Obj-based:** Properties of an object can be modified at run-time; Built-in functions are used for properties to maintain dynamicity

c) **Run-time evaluation:** eval() is used for run time evaluation and will take dynamic arguments at run time

This page is intentionally left blank

Opening and Manipulating Windows

113: How can you open a new window using JavaScript?
Answer:
We can open a new web browser window using "open()" method of the Window object.Window.open() has four optional arguments and returns a window object that represents the new open window. The first argument is the URL of the document to display in the new window (if it is null or empty string, the window will be empty), the second argument is the name of the window; the third parameter is a list of features that specify the window size and GUI decoration. The fourth argument is useful only when the second argument is mentioned.

114: How can you close a window using JavaScript?
Answer:
We can close a created window object using "close()" method. The syntax is: Window.close()

115: What does the "location" function do in JavaScript?
Answer:
The location property of a window is a reference to a location object and represents the URL of the document that is displayed in the window. The Href property of the location object is a string that contains all the text of the URL.

116: What other properties besides Href can we find in the "location" function in JavaScript?
Answer:
Other properties that we can use are: protocol, host, pathname and search.

117: What happens when a string value is added to the location function in JavaScript?
Answer:
The browser interprets the string as a URL and tries to load it and display the document and that URL.

118: What is the history object in JavaScript?
Answer:
The history object refers to the History of the browser window. The multitudes of elements that the history object incorporates are never accessible to scripts.

119: Which are the methods supported by the history object in JavaScript?
Answer:
There are three methods supported by the history object: the back(), the forward() and the go().

120: How many and which are the coordinates of a browser within the HTML document?
Answer:
There are three types of coordinates and these are: screen, window and document coordinates.

This page is intentionally left blank

Objects and their Properties in JavaScript

121: What is the screen object in JavaScript?
Answer:
The screen property of a Window refers to a screen object that provides information about the user's display and the number of colors that are available on it.

122: What is the Navigator object in JavaScript?
Answer:
The navigator property of a Window refers to a navigator object that contains information about the whole web browser such as the version of it.

123: Name the properties of Navigator in JavaScript.
Answer:
There are five properties for the navigator object and these are: appName, appVersion, userAgent, appCodeName and platform.

124: What happens when confirm() or prompt() methods are used in JavaScript?
Answer:
When these boxes are initialized the code stops running and the currently loading document stops loading until the user response with the requested input.

125: What happens when the mouse is moved over a hyperlink in JavaScript?
Answer:
JavaScript code evaluates the onmouseover attribute and sets the status property of the window, thus returning the "true" value telling the browser not to take any actions.

126: What does the "defaultStatus" property do in JavaScript?
Answer:
The "defaultStatus" property enables text to be displayed in the status line when the browser does not find anything to display. Newer versions of the current browser have this property

deprecated.

127: What is the "onerror" property in JavaScript?
Answer:
The "onerror" property has a special status: the function the user assigns becomes an error handler for the window; the function assigned to the property is invoked when an error occurs in that window.

128: What arguments does the error handler receive when an error occurs in JavaScript?
Answer:
The error handler receives three arguments: the first is the message that describes the error; the second is the string that contains the URL of the document containing the JavaScript code that caused the error and the third argument is line number within the document where the error occurred.

129: In addition to the three arguments that the error handler receives, is its return value of any importance?
Answer:
The return value of the error handler is significant: if the onerror handler returns True then the browser does not display its own error message having been told that the handler has taken care of the error.

130: How can JavaScript code can refer to a window or frame object?
Answer:
In JavaScript we can refer in any window or frame to its own window or frame using "window" or "self". They are necessary to use when the programmer needs to refer to this global object itself. In case the programmer wants to refer to a method or property of the window/frame, it is not necessary to prefix the property or method name with "window" or "self".

131: What is a DOM (Document Object Model)?

Answer:

DOM (Document Object Model) is an API that defines the way to access the objects that compose a document. W3C defines a standard DOM that is reasonably well supported in all modern browsers.

132: What does the method write() of the Document object do?

Answer:

The write() method allows users to write content into the document. The write() method is part of DOM and it can be used in two ways. First of all, it can be used within a script to output HTML into the document being parsed. Second, write() can be used (in conjunction with open() and close() methods of the Document object) to create entirely new documents in other windows or frames.

133: How will you determine an object type?

Answer:

Using "Instanceof and isprototypeof" by checking its instance and prototype respectively.
Example: document.writeln(book1 instanceof Book);
var Book = function() {...};
Book.prototype.constructor == Book; //return true.

134: What is alert and confirm box in java script?

Answer:
   a) Alert and confirm both are pop ups in JavaScript and take the focus of the user from the current page to pop ups
   b) Alert provides the user with "ok" button whereas confirm provides with "ok" and "cancel" button where user can select any one of the options
   c) When "ok" is selected, confirm returns true else false

135: What are the properties of array object?

Answer:

a) Index property
b) Input property
c) Length property
d) Constructor property
e) Prototype property

136: What are the sub objects of the windows object in JavaScript?
Answer:
a) **Document object:** Work with DOM and provides interface to XML and Html documents and allow CSS manipulations
b) **Frame object:** Represents <frame> HTML frames. Frame object will be created for each <frame> tag
c) **Location object:** Contains the current URL information "window.location"
d) **History object:** Contains the URL history visited by the user

137: What is the use of userAgent of navigator object?
Answer:
a) Identifies the operating system of the client's machine
b) "appVersion" and "userAgent" can also be used
c) "userAgent" property of navigator object returns the value of the user agent header sent by the browser to server

Syntax:
document.write(navigator.userAgent);
document.write(navigator.appVersion);

138: What are the ways to delete the property of an object and how?
Answer:
It can be deleted in two ways.
Example:
oven=new Object();

```
oven.name="LG";
oven.color="Black";
```

a) using object name and property
   example: delete oven.color;
b) using object name and property with "with"statement
   example: with(oven)
        delete color;

139: What is the use of eval() in JSON?
Answer:
JSON can be parsed using the built-in function eval() and JSON data is executed to generate native JavaScript object.
Example:
```
obj_json2=eval('(' + JSON_text+')');
```

140: What are the advantages of JSON over XML?
Answer:
a) JSON provides array and object type and also some scalar data types whereas XML does not provide any data types
b) Formatting is done by direct mapping in JSON whereas it is complex in Xml
c) Document size is too large in XML. When the data grows, amount of xml also grows whereas documents are compact in JSON

XML:
```
<Record>
    <First_Name>abcd</First_Name>
    <Age>25</Age>
</Record>
```

JSON:
```
{
"Record":{"First_Name":"abcd","Age":"25"}
}
```

141: How can the properties of JavaScript objects be accessed?
Answer:
In thebelow two ways, the properties of Javascript objects be accessed:
Syntax:
    a) obj_name.prop1;
    b) obj_name["prop1"];

142: What are the objects of navigator objects?
Answer:
    a) **Window object:** gets created for every frame and web browser
    b) **Mime type object:** using enabledplugin, gets information about the plugin
    c) **Plugin object:** gives information about an installed plug-in

143: How to access the properties of the main window from secondary window?
Answer:
Using Opener property. The properties of the main window can be accessed from secondary window.
Example:
In the secondary window:
window.opener.document.bgColor="my_color_value"; //give color name or hex code

It changes the background color of the primary window to the given color.

144: How will you load the previous and next url from the history list?
Answer:
Using back and forward function of history object, the previous and next url from the history list can be loaded.
Example:

"history.back()";
"history.forward()";

145: How will you determine whether the browser has cookies enabled?

Answer:
Using cookieEnabled function of navigator object, the browser status can be determined. If cookies are enabled returns true, else false.

Example:
If(navigator.cookieEnabled)
    document.write("Enabled");
else
    document.write("Not Enabled");

JavaScript and HTML

146: How can you change the font size of an Element in JavaScript? Give an example.
Answer:
document.getElementById(elementId).style.fontSize = "12"; In this case, JavaScript and CSS are very similar, because the CSS style rules are laid on top of the DOM.

147: How can you submit a form using JavaScript?
Answer:
This can be done using document.form[0].submit(), where 0 represent the index of the form in the page. If there are more than one form in the page, then the first form has index 0, the second form has index 1 and so on.

148: How can you set the background color of an HMTL document?
Answer:
This can be easily done using document.bgcolor = "color", where color can be the name of a color – e.g. red, black, or it can represent the code of the color – e.g. #00FF34.

149: Name the Boolean operators in JavaScript.
Answer:
The Boolean operators in JavaScript are: '&&' - AND operator, ' | | ' – OR operator '!' - NOT operator.

150: How can we determine the state of a checkbox in JavaScript?
Answer:
var isChecked = window.document.getElementById(elementId).checked – isChecked is the name of the variable where the true or false value will be stored. ElementId represents the id of the checkbox element. If the checkbox is checked this will return true, otherwise false.

151: How can you create an HTML button and what is the event called when the button is pressed?
Answer:
An HTML button can be create like this: <input type="button"> or <button type="button"> and the event is "onclick"

152: How will you make loading of JavaScript code after Html by the browser?
Answer:
By "defer" script we can load Javascript code after Html. It informs the browser to load all html codes before JavaScript. So the code inside the defer script gets executed only when the page is entirely parsed. It can use on both external and inline scripts.
Example:
<script type='text/javascript' src='a1.js' defer='defer'></script>

Here loading of a1.js takes place after all html code has been parsed.

153: Which popup allows the user to enter the input?
Answer:
Prompt box allows the user to enter the input. It provides the user with text box for input and two buttons ("ok and cancel"). On selecting "Ok", it returns true otherwise false.
Example:
var a1= prompt("content1","myDefault_val");

154: What are the ways to display the message on screen?
Answer:
   a) Using write method.
       Eg: document.write("hello");
   b) Using getElementById.
       Eg: function disp(text) {
             var m1 = document.getElementById("my_disp");
             m1.innerHTML = text;
             return true;

}

155: How will you reload the page from server using JavaScript?
Answer:
Using reload() we can reload a page. It is a function of location object that contains the details of present url. It takes either true or false as argument. Default argument is false. When set to false, reloads the page from cache. Otherwise ask the browser to load the page from server.
Syntax:
Window.location.reload(value);

156: How will you display large tables effectively in JavaScript?
Answer:
Using fixed width table we can display large tables effectively. Fixed width tables are provided by the browser based on the width of the columns in the first row, ensuring faster display. Advantage: No need for the browser to wait till all data is received to infer the best width.
Syntax:
In css,set "table-layout:fixed"

157: How will you create pop window using JavaScript?
Answer:
It can be created as below:
  a) **window.open():** opens a new browser window
      Syntax:
      Window.open(page_Url, window_
      name,properties,replace);
      For pop window,replace is always set to false.
  b) **window.showDialogBox():** creates a modal dialog box
      Syntax:
      window.showDialogBox(page_url,window_name,properti
      es);

158: How will you fix the errors that make the JavaScript

engines difficult to perform optimization?
Answer:
Using "Strict Mode" which makes the code run faster than the code without strict mode such errors could be fixed. To enable strict mode, insert 'use strict mode' before the code. It takes care of following functions:
a) Duplications are not allowed
b) If Deprecated languages is used, throws error
c) It denounces 'with' statement
d) Assign to read-only variables are not allowed

159: How will you make secure JavaScript code?
Answer:
a) Using Strict Mode. The value passed with the "this" (keyword) to a function will not be changed in strict mode
b) When a function is in strict mode, fn_name.arguments and fn_name.caller throws error when tried to get or set

160: How will you add the external JavaScript file?
Answer:
External JavaScript file should be saved with an extension ".js" and needs to be imported to the html file by adding that file's path to the "src" attribute of <script> tag.
Example:
<html>
<head>
    <script src="aa.js"></script>
</head>
<body>...</body>
</html>

161: Is it possible to break up a string in a JavaScript code?
Answer:
Yes. Using backslash"\", a text can break up in a code.
Example:
document.write("Break \

up a code");
⟶ document.write \
("Cannot break like this"); // This is not possible.

162: What is the use of "wait" property in cursor style?
Answer:
Wait sets the cursor in wait state when the request is on process.
Type of cursor can be set or returned by using "cursor property".
Some of the type of cursor are:
  a) **default:** default cursor
  b) **wait:** loading symbol or hourglass
  c) **auto:** browser default cursor
  d) **help:** arrow with a question mark symbol

Syntax:
myobject.style.cursor="my_value";
eg:myobject-window,document, my_value-wait,auto,help...

163: What are the properties that can be set in the background properties?
Answer:
  a) **color:** sets the bgcolor
  b) **image:** sets the bgimage
  c) **repeat:** repeats the bgimage
  d) **attachment:** makes the image fixed or scrolls with the page
  e) **position:** sets the starting position of an image

Syntax:
my_object.style.background="my_value";
    // my_object=>window,document,..
    // my_value=>color,image,reappear,attachment,position

164: What are the ways to set the background color?
Answer:
In the following two ways:
  a) Using bgColor

> my_obj.bgcolor="my_color"
>   my_obj $\longrightarrow$ document
>   my_color $\longrightarrow$ colors,color value
> b) Using background
>   my_obj.style.backgroundColor="my_value";
>   my_obj $\longrightarrow$ document
>   my_value=color,image,reappear,attachment,position

165: How will you add JavaScript files dynamically?
Answer:
By creating a new script element file and append it to the document, we can add Javascript files dynamically
Example:
var head_elemt=document.getElementByTagName("...."); //pass tag name like"head"
var my_script=document.createElement('...'); //pass type as script
my_script.type='text/javascript';
my_script.src='www.abc.co/ab.js';
head_elemt.appendChild(my_script);

166: How will you get the current "x and y" co-ordinate value of the window when it is scrolled?
Answer:
a) Using onscroll. It executes when the window is scrolled
b) pageXOffset and pageYOffset are used to get the co-ordinate value

Example:
window.onscroll=function(){
var xvalue=window.pageXOffset ;
document.write(xvalue);}

167: What are the methods to create remote window?
Answer:
a) Using custom property
   Secondary window:

```
windw2=window.open("remote_win2");
windw2.maker=self; //"self" gives the current window
```
Remote window:
```
function remote_wind2(link2){
    maker.location=link2;
}
<input type="button" value="Address"
onclick=remote_wind2()>
```
b) Using opener property
```
function remote_windw2(link1){
    window.opener.location=link;
}
<input type="button" value="Address"
onclick=remote_windw2()>
```

168: How will you get the height of the browser window?
Answer:
a) Using availHeight property of the screen object.
b) Gives the height of the browser window excluding the taskbar height,etc..

Example:
```
document.write("Height:" + screen.availHeight);
```

169: How will you get the language code of the linked page?
Answer:
Using hreflang property of the anchor object we can get the language code of the linked page. Anchor object creates a link to another page or document.
Example:
```
my_anchor_object1.hreflang;
```

170: How would you input a file?
Answer:
Using FileUpload Object we can input a file. The type should be specified as "file" in the <input> tag. It creates the fileupload

object that opens the file dialog box on clicking the button.
Example:
<input type="file" >

This page is intentionally left blank

JavaScript Forms

171: What is the importance of the "name" attribute of a <form> tag?

Answer:

When a Form object is created, the name attribute is stored as an element in the form[] array of the Document object, and it is also stored in the properties of the Document objects. So, after defining a <form name="formName">, it will be easy to refer the Form object using document.formName instead of document.form[0]. This attribute has nothing to do with submitting the form.

172: What are the event handlers of the form element?

Answer:

The following event handlers are supported by form elements: onclick, onchange, onfocus, onblur.

173: What does "onchange" event handler do?

Answer:

This event handler is triggered when the user enters text or selects an option, changing in this way the value represented by the element. Button and other related elements do not support this event handler because they don't have a value that can be edited. This event it is triggered when the focus is lost and it is moved to another form element.

174: What is a "cookie"?

Answer:

A cookie is a named data stored by the web browser and associated with a particular web page or web site. They were originally designed for the server-side programming and they are implemented as an extension to the HTTP protocol. The cookie data is transmitted between the client and the server and the server-side scripts can read and write cookie values that are stored on the client. In JavaScript, cookies are manipulated using "cookie" property of the Document object.

175: What does the "new" operator do?

Answer:

The "new" operator creates a new object, that has no properties, and then it invokes the function passing the new objected created as the value of "this" keyword. The function that uses the "new" operator is called "constructor function" or just simply "constructor".

176: What does <optgroup> tag do in JavaScript?

Answer:

It is used with select statement to group the related options in the drop down list. It will be useful to display long list

Example:

```
<select>
    <optgroup label="JAVA">
<option value="hibernate1">Hibernate</option>
<option value="struts1"> Struts </option>
    </optgroup>
    <optgroup label="WEBSERVICE">
        <option value="soap1">SOAP</option>
        <option value="xml1"> Xml </option>
    </optgroup>
</select>
```

177: Comparison between session state and view state.

Answer:

Functions	Session State	View State
Maintenance	Session level-data of user sessions	Page level maintenance-state of page
Visibility	State value available to all pages within the user's session	State value of one page is not visible to another page
Storage	State information stored in server	State information stored in client
Data	Permanently store the user specific data in server	Permanently store the page instance specific data in client

178: Which function is best for fast execution: window.onload or onDocumentReady?

Answer:
a) window.onDocumentReady
b) Because it executes the code once DOM is loaded by the browser and will not wait for the object such as images to be loaded
c) Whereas onLoad executes only when the browser loads DOM and all other resources such as images gets loaded

179: What is the purpose of "visibility" property in JavaScript?

Answer:
a) **"Visibility"**: Makes the element either visible or invisible
b) **"collapse"**: Used to hide the elements in a table
c) **"inherit"**: Takes the values from the parent element

Example:
my_elemt.style.visibility="my_val";
my_val $\longrightarrow$ visible,hidden,collapse,inherit

180: What are the ways to make an element visible/hidden?

Answer:
a) Using display property
    my_elemt.style.display=" "; //visible
    my_elemt.style.display="none"; //hidden
b) Using visibility property
    my_elemt.style.visibility="visible"; //visible
    my_elemt.style.visibility="hidden"; //hidden

181: How will you disable the html form fields, for instance password field?

Answer:
Using disabled property of a password object.
Example:
document.getElementById("Field_Id").disabled=true;

182: How will you select the contents in the text field, say password?

Answer:

Using select function of password object, we can select the contents in text field.

Example:

document.getElementById("Field_Id").select();

183: How will you display the id of the form and the name attribute of the hidden element?

Answer:

Using "form" and name property of hidden object, we can display the id of the form and the name attribute of the hidden element

Example:

var form_id1=
document.getElementById("my_elemt_id").form.id;
var name_id2= document.getElementById("my_elemt_id").name;

184: How will you get the last row from a table in JavaScript?

Answer:

Using tFoot property of a table object we can get the last row from a table. The last rows of tables in Html can be combined using the tfoot element.

Example:

my_table_objects.tFoot;
my_table_objects ⟶ document object,getElementById property

185: How will you create and delete caption to a table?

Answer:

Using createCaption and deleteCaption function of the table object.

Example:

my_table_objects.createCaption(); //create
my_table_objects.deleteCaption(); //delete
my_table_objects ⟶ document object,getElementById

property

186: How will you create a text area and make it read-only?
Answer:
  a) Using textarea object
     Example:
     <textarea id="my_txt" cols="22">
     My_text
     </textarea>
  b) Using readOnly property of textarea object
     Example:
     my_table_objects.readOnly="my_value1"; //delete
        my_table_objects ──➤ document
        object,getElementById property
        my_value1 ──➤ true

187: How will you change the caption display position of a table?
Answer:
Using captionSide property of the style object we can change the caption display position of a table.
Example:
my_obj1.style.captionSide="values";
    my_obj1 ──➤ document object,getElementById property
    values ──➤ top/bottom

JavaScript Constructors

188: What does a JavaScript constructor do?

Answer:

The constructor initializes the newly created object and sets any properties that need to be set before that object is used. You can easily define a constructor function, by writing a function that adds properties to "this" operator.

Example:

```
// define the constructor
function circle(r){
this.radius = r;
}
//invoke the constructor to create a circle object:
var circle1 = new circle(3); // we pass the radius value to the
constructor so that it will initialize the new object appropriately.
```

189: What is the value that the constructor function returns?

Answer:

Typically, the constructor does not return any values. They simply initialize the object passed as the value of "this" operator and return nothing. Anyway, the constructor can return an object value, but in this case the returned object becomes the value of the "new" expression and the object that was the value of this is simply not taken into account.

190: How many types of common object methods can we find in JavaScript?

Answer:

We have three types of object methods: the toString|() method; the valueOf() method and comparison method.

191: How does class hierarchy manifest themselves in JavaScript?

Answer:

Java and C++ have an explicit concept of the class hierarchy; so any class can be extended or sub-classed so that subclass that results can be inherited. JavaScript supports prototype inheritance instead of class-based inheritance so the Object class is the most generic with all other classes as specialized versions of it or subclasses.

192: What does "overriding method" mean?
Answer:
If a subclass defines a method that has the same name as the method in the superclass it is called overriding that method. This is a common thing to do when creating subclasses of existing classes. For example when toString() method is defined, the toString() method of Object is overridden.

193: How can you create an XML document in Firefox using JavaScript?
Answer:
We can create an empty XML Document in Firefox and related browsers with document.implementation.createDocument() which is a DOM Level 2 method.

194: How are images accessed from JavaScript?
Answer:
Images can be referred using document.images[0] // for the first images, document.images[1] and so one for the next images. Once the image is accessed, you can perform different tasks on them.

195: Where is the arguments() array placed in JavaScript?
Answer:
It is placed and defined only within a function body. Within the arguments of a body arguments refers to Arguments object for the function.

196: Which are the properties of the arguments object in JavaScript?
Answer:
The properties of the arguments object are callee and length. All values that are passed as arguments become array elements of the

arguments object.

197: What happens when a function is invoked with the arguments object?

Answer:

Arguments object is created for it and the local variable arguments are initialized to refer that arguments object.

Miscellaneous Arguments, Functions and Methods in JavaScript

198: What does arguments.callee do in JavaScript?

Answer:

The arguments.callee refers to the currently running function and it provides a way for an unnamed function to refer to itself.

199: What does arguments.length do in JavaScript?

Answer:

The arguments.length specifies the number of arguments that are passed to the current function; it only specifies the number of arguments actually passed and not the expected number.

200: What other JavaScript method you know that is similar with shift() method?

Answer:

Other method similar with shift() is Array.pop(), the only exception is that it operates on the beginning of an array rather that the end.

201: How can you remove a page from the browser history?

Answer:

If the programmer wants to remove the current page from the browser history, it can simply use location.replace() method. Invoking this method causes the browser to request a page through a GET method just like a regular web page.

202: How can you pass data between pages using cookies?

Answer:

In this case cookies.js library can be used with onunload event handler of one page to store 1 to 20 name/value pairs on the user's machine. In the second document, the onload event handler is used to retrieve the cookie data and assign the value to a text input field with the same name located on the second page.

203: What is the difference between resizeTo() and resizeBy() methods?

Answer:

Both the given methods are applicable to window object. In case you want to resize the window to a specific pixel size, resizeTo() method is the most appropriate. To increase or decrease the size of the window by a fixed pixel amount, you can use resizeBy() method.

204: What's the difference between moveTo() and moveBy() methods?

Answer:
Both the methods are applicable to window object. The first method, moveTo() is used to move the window to a screen coordinate point, by the other hand, the moveby() method shifts the position of the window by a known pixel amount.

205: How can a window that is buried beneath other windows be brought back to the front?

Answer:
In this case, for any window to which you have a valid reference, the focus() method must be invoked.

206: What happens when a string argument is passed with the Date() constructor in JavaScript?

Answer:
If one string argument passes with the Date() constructor it results in the string being a representation of a date in the format that is accepted by the Date.parse() method.

207: Which are the arguments of the Date() constructor in JavaScript?

Answer:
The date() constructor arguments are: milliseconds1, datestring, year, month, day, hours, minutes, seconds and milliseconds2 (optional argument).

208: What does URIError indicate in JavaScript?

Answer:

The URIError indicates that one or more escape sequences in URI are malformed and they cannot be correctly sequenced.

209: What does the encodeURIComponent function do in JavaScript?
Answer:
It is a global function that returns an encoded copy of the string argument.

210: What does the string argument do in JavaScript?
Answer:
The string argument is a string that simply contains a portion of a URI or other text that has to be encoded.

211: What is and what does the escape() function do in JavaScript?
Answer:
The escape() function is a global function that returns a new string that contains an encoded version of s; the string s by itself is not modified.

212: What does the apply() function do in JavaScript and which are its arguments?
Answer:
The apply() function invokes the specified function and treats it like it were a method of thisobj argument passing it then the arguments contained by the args array.

213: What does the getClass() function do in JavaScript?
Answer:
The getClass() function takes a JavaObject object as an argument and return the JavaClass object of the respective JavaObject.

214: What is Infinity in JavaScript?
Answer:
Infinity is a global property that contains special numeric value

that represents positive infinity; it cannot be deleted by the delete operator.

215: What does the exec() method do in JavaScript?
Answer:
The exec() is the most powerful pattern-matching method of RegExp and String. It searches string for text that matches the regexp and if it finds a match returns an array of results; if not it returns null.

216: What happens when the exec() method is invoked on a nonglobal pattern?
Answer:
The exec() performs a search and then returns the same result as String.match() would.

217: Does exec() include full details of every match even if regexp is not global?
Answer:
It is different in this regard to String.match() which return less information when used with global patterns.

218: What is an anchor in JavaScript?
Answer:
An anchor is a named location within an Html document that is created with an <a> tag that has an attribute specified.

219: What does the focus() method do in JavaScript?
Answer:
The focus() method scrolls the document so that the anchor location is visible; it is created by any standard HTML <a> tag that contains a name attribute.

220: Is JSObject a JavaScript object?
Answer:
No. JSObject is a Java class that cannot be used in any JavaScript

programs; it invokes the JavaScript methods into Java.

221: What does the call() method of JSObject class do?
Answer:
It invokes a name method of the JavaScript object represented by the JSObject; the arguments are passed to the method as an array of Java objects, then the return value of the JavaScript method is returned as a Java object.

222: What does the eval() method of the JSObject do?
Answer:
It evaluates the JavaScript code that is contained within a string s in the context of the JavaScript object. Its behavior is similar to that of the eval() method of JavaScript.

223: What does the getSlot() method of the JSObject do?
Answer:
It reads and returns the value of an array element that is specified at the index of a JavaScript object.

224: What does the removeMember() method of the JSObject do?
Answer:
It deletes a named property that belongs to the JavaScript object represented by the JSObject.

225: What does the setMember() method of the JSObject do?
Answer:
This method is the opposite of removeMember in that it sets a value of a named property of a JavaScript object from Java.

226: What does the toString() method of JSObject do?
Answer:
It invokes the toString() of the JavaScript object and returns the result of that method.

227: What does the (n) argument represent in isFinite(n) and what does it return?

Answer:
The (n) argument is the number that is to be tested and if n can be converted or is a finite number return true and false or NaN if n is positive or negative infinity.

228: What does the isNaN() function do in JavaScript?

Answer:
It tests its arguments to see if it is the value of Nan, which is an illegal number.

229: What does the setYear() function do in JavaScript?

Answer:
It sets the year field of a specified date object with a special behavior for years between 1900 and 1999.

230: What does the join() method do in JavaScript?

Answer:
Put in all the elements of the array into a string separed by the specified separator. Default separartor is comma ",".
Example:
var fourwheelers = ["Car","Bus","Lorry"] ;
document.write(fourwheelers.join("-")); ⟶ "Car-Bus-Lorry"

231: How will you pop the last element from an existing array?

Answer:
Using pop() function we can pop the last elemnt from an existing array. It removes and returns the last element of an array. Length of the array will decrease by 1.
Example:
var no=[1,2,3];
document.write(no); ⟶ "1,2,3"
document.write.(no.pop() +"<br>"); ⟶ "3"
document.write(no); ⟶ "1,2"

232: How to pop the first element from an existing array?
Answer:
Using shift() function we can pop the first element from an existing array. It removes and returns the first element of an array. Length of the array will decrease by 1.
Example:
```
var no=[1,2,3];
document.write(no);   ——▶  "1,2,3"
document.write.(no.shift() +"<br>");   ——▶  "1"
document.write(no);   ——▶  "2,3"
```

233: How will you add one or more elements to the end of the existing array?
Answer:
Using push() function we can add more elents. It adds the new items to the end of the array and returns its length.
Example:
```
var no=[1,2,3];
document.write(no);   ——▶  "1,2,3"
document.write(no.push(5));   ——▶  "4"
document.write(no);   ——▶  "1,2,3,5"
```

234: How will you add one or more elements to the beginning of the existing array?
Answer:
Using unshift() function we can add more elements. It adds the new items to the begining of the array and returns its length.
Example:
```
var no=[1,2,3];
document.write(no);   ——▶  "1,2,3"
document.write(no. unshift (5));   ——▶  "4"
document.write(no);   ——▶  "5,1,2,3"
```

235: How will you reverse the elements in an array?
Answer:
Using reverse() function without creating new array.

Example:
var no=[1,2,3];
document.write(no); ⟶ "1,2,3"
document.write(no.reverse()); ⟶ "3,2,1"

236: What does the Array.slice(start,end) method do in JavaScript and how to retrieve the elements within the selected position in an array?
Answer:
Its returns the array object containing the elements starting from the specified start value till the element before the end value. When a negative value is used for the start or end values, that gets added to the length of the array and returns the elements within that position.

237: What does the Array.sort() method do in JavaScript?
Answer:
  a) **Default sort():** used to sort the alphabets in ascending order
  b) **reverse() is used with the sort():** Used to sort the alphabets in descending order
  c) **To sort the numbers,** some functions are passed as arguments in sort()

238: What is encodeURI( ) and encodeURIComponent( )?
Answer:
  a) Used to encode the given uri
  b) encodeURI() encodes the special characters except " : @ $ # = & / + ? "
  a) c) encodeURIComponent encodes all the special characters including " : @ $ # = & / + ? "

239: What is decodeURI( ) and decodeURIComponent( )?
Answer:
  a) Used to decode the given encoded uri. decodeURI() decodes the special characters except " : @ $ # = & / + ? "

b) decodeURIComponent denotes all the special characters including " : @ $ # = & / + ? "

240: What does the splice( ) function do in JavaScript?
Answer:
Adds or remove elements to/from an existing array and return the removed elements.
array.splice(index,no of items to be removed,new items1,new items2...new itemn);

Example:
var no=[1,2,3,4,5];
document.write(no); ⟶ "1,2,3,4,5"
document.write(no. splice (1,2,9,10)); ⟶ "2,3"
document.write(no); ⟶ "1,9,10,4,5"

241: How will you print the current window using JavaScript?
Answer:
Using window.print() function to print the contents of the specified window.

242: How will you get default value when an argument is not passed in calling function?
Answer:
By Shorthand assignment. It checks whether the passed argument contains a value.
Example:
function add1(a1,a2){
    var b1=a1 || 1; ⟶ b1=5
    var b2=a2 || 2; ⟶ b2=2
    return b1+b2; ⟶ 7
}
add1(5);

Here, since the first argument is only passed, it is treated as true hence"5" gets assigned to b1. Since the Second argument is not passed, it is treated as undefined value (i.e.) false hence the default value gets assigned.

243: How will you encode and decode a string?
Answer:
a) **Using escape() and unescape()**
b) **escape():** Encodes the string and special characters except " + * - _ . @ / " . It converts the non Ascii codes to two or four digit hex format
c) **unescape():** decodes the encoded string

244: How will you pass a function as argument to another function?
Answer:
Using callback. A function that is passed as a argument to another function gets a reference called "Callback". The callback functions gets executed only after the execution of called function.
Example:

```
function  oven(time,callback){
    document.write("Started at" +time+ "<br>");
    callback();
}

oven(5,function(){
    document.write("Stopped");});
```

Output:
Started at 5
Stopped

245: What is the need for callback function?
Answer:
When a function is called, execution of the function takes place which will return some value. If the execution time will be longer for the function to return a value, for instance, when it may have to wait for some input from another function or user, it needs to

be implemented asynchronously using callback function.

246: How will you get a substring from a string in JavaScript?
Answer:
a) **substring():** Retrieves the string starting from the start value till end value. White space are included
   Syntax: substring(start_value,end_value);
b) **substr():** Retrieves the string starting from the start value till the length specified
   Syntax: substr(start_value,leng);

Example:
var a="color my world";
document.write(substring(3,7);   // r my
document.write(substr(3,7);   // o my wo

247: How will you get the function (fn1) which recently called the current function (fn2)?
Answer:
Using "fn2.caller" we can get the fn1 info. If the control of the program is in the fn2(), it will return the function (fn1) by which fn2 is recently called by using fn2.caller.
"fn2.arguments" gives the arguments passed to the fn2.
Example:
```
function fn_2(){
    use strict mode;
    fn_2.caller;
    fn_2.arguments;
}
function fn_1(){
fn_2();
}
```

248: How will you execute the page that is about to be unloaded, before the execution of onload()?
Answer:

Using onbeforeunload we can execute the page that is about to be unloaded. The "onunload" function occurs when the page is closed or navigating to another page. Hence onbeforeunload alerts the user about navigation before "onunload".

Example:

```
window.onbeforeunload=alert_msg();
function alert_msg(){
    return "Message to be displayed to the user.";
}
```

249: How will you find whether the window is closed or not?

Answer:

Using closed property we can check the status of the window. It returns "true" if the window is closed else returns "false".

Example:

```
if(window.opener.closed)
    document.write("closed");
else
    document.write("open");
```

250: How will you call a function repeatedly for a particular interval of time?

Answer:

Using setInterval function we can repeatedly call a function for a period of time.. It also clears the timer by returning unique id which will be passed as a parameter for clearTimer.

Example:

```
setInterval(my_funct_1(),444);
my_funct_1  ⟶ function to be called
444  ⟶ specified_ interval
```

251: What is the difference between test and exec function?

Answer:

a) Both functions are used to search the particular pattern.

b) test function returns a Boolean value and exec function returns the found value.

This page is intentionally left blank

HR Questions

*Review these typical interview questions and think about how you
ould answer them. Read the answers listed; you will find best
possible answers along with strategies and suggestions.*

1: Would you rather receive more authority or more responsibility at work?

Answer:

There are pros and cons to each of these options, and your interviewer will be more interested to see that you can provide a critical answer to the question. Receiving more authority may mean greater decision-making power and may be great for those with outstanding leadership skills, while greater responsibility may be a growth opportunity for those looking to advance steadily throughout their careers.

2: What do you do when someone in a group isn't contributing their fair share?

Answer:

This is a particularly important question if you're interviewing for a position in a supervisory role – explain the ways in which you would identify the problem, and how you would go about pulling aside the individual to discuss their contributions. It's important to understand the process of creating a dialogue, so that you can communicate your expectations clearly to the individual, give them a chance to respond, and to make clear what needs to change. After this, create an action plan with the group member to ensure their contributions are on par with others in the group.

3: Tell me about a time when you made a decision that was outside of your authority.

Answer:

While an answer to this question may portray you as being decisive and confident, it could also identify you to an employer as a potential problem employee. Instead, it may be best to slightly refocus the question into an example of a time that you took on additional responsibilities, and thus had to make decisions that were outside of your normal authority (but which had been granted to you in the specific instance). Discuss how the weight of the decision affected your decision-making process, and the outcomes of the situation.

4: Are you comfortable going to supervisors with disputes?
Answer:
If a problem arises, employers want to know that you will handle it in a timely and appropriate manner. Emphasize that you've rarely had disputes with supervisors in the past, but if a situation were to arise, you feel perfectly comfortable in discussing it with the person in question in order to find a resolution that is satisfactory to both parties.

5: If you had been in charge at your last job, what would you have done differently?
Answer:
No matter how many ideas you have about how things could run better, or opinions on the management at your previous job, remain positive when answering this question. It's okay to show thoughtful reflection on how something could be handled in order to increase efficiency or improve sales, but be sure to keep all of your suggestions focused on making things better, rather than talking about ways to eliminate waste or negativity.

6: Do you believe employers should praise or reward employees for a job well done?
Answer:
Recognition is always great after completing a difficult job, but there are many employers who may ask this question as a way to infer as to whether or not you'll be a high-maintenance worker. While you may appreciate rewards or praise, it's important to convey to the interviewer that you don't require accolades to be confident that you've done your job well. If you are interviewing for a supervisory position where you would be the one praising other employees, highlight the importance of praise in boosting team morale.

7: What do you believe is the most important quality a leader can have?
Answer:

There are many important skills for a leader to have in any business, and the most important component of this question is that you explain why the quality you choose to highlight is important. Try to choose a quality such as communication skills, or an ability to inspire people, and relate it to a specific instance in which you displayed the quality among a team of people.

8: Tell me about a time when an unforeseen problem arose. How did you handle it?
Answer:
It's important that you are resourceful, and level-headed under pressure. An interviewer wants to see that you handle problems systematically, and that you can deal with change in an orderly process. Outline the situation clearly, including all solutions and results of the process you implemented.

9: Can you give me an example of a time when you were able to improve X *objective* at your previous job?
Answer:
It's important here to focus on an improvement you made that created tangible results for your company. Increasing efficiency is certainly a very important element in business, but employers are also looking for concrete results such as increased sales or cut expenses. Explain your process thoroughly, offering specific numbers and evidence wherever possible, particularly in outlining the results.

10: Tell me about a time when a supervisor did not provide specific enough direction on a project.
Answer:
While many employers want their employees to follow very specific guidelines without much decision-making power, it's important also to be able to pick up a project with vague direction and to perform self-sufficiently. Give examples of necessary questions that you asked, and specify how you determined whether a question was something you needed to ask of a

supervisor or whether it was something you could determine on your own.

11: Tell me about a time when you were in charge of leading a project.
Answer:
Lead the interviewer through the process of the project, just as you would have with any of your team members. Explain the goal of the project, the necessary steps, and how you delegated tasks to your team. Include the results, and what you learned as a result of the leadership opportunity.

12: Tell me about a suggestion you made to a former employer that was later implemented.
Answer:
Employers want to see that you're interested in improving your company and doing your part – offer a specific example of something you did to create a positive change in your previous job. Explain how you thought of the idea, how your supervisors received it, and what other employees thought was the idea was put into place.

13: Tell me about a time when you thought of a way something in the workplace could be done more efficiently.
Answer:
Focus on the positive aspects of your idea. It's important not to portray your old company or boss negatively, so don't elaborate on how inefficient a particular system was. Rather, explain a situation in which you saw an opportunity to increase productivity or to streamline a process, and explain in a general step-by-step how you implemented a better system.

14: Is there a difference between leading and managing people – which is your greater strength?
Answer:
There is a difference – leaders are often great idea people,

passionate, charismatic, and with the ability to organize and inspire others, while managers are those who ensure a system runs, facilitate its operations, make authoritative decisions, and who take great responsibility for all aspects from overall success to the finest decisions. Consider which of these is most applicable to the position, and explain how you fit into this role, offering concrete examples of your past experience.

15: Do you function better in a leadership role, or as a worker on a team?
Answer:
It is important to consider what qualities the interviewer is looking for in your position, and to express how you embody this role. If you're a leader, highlight your great ideas, drive and passion, and ability to incite others around you to action. If you work great in teams, focus on your dedication to the task at hand, your cooperation and communication skills, and your ability to keep things running smoothly.

16: Tell me about a time when you discovered something in the workplace that was disrupting your (or others) productivity – what did you do about it?
Answer:
Try to not focus on negative aspects of your previous job too much, but instead choose an instance in which you found a positive, and quick, solution to increase productivity. Focus on the way you noticed the opportunity, how you presented a solution to your supervisor, and then how the change was implemented (most importantly, talk about how you led the change initiative). This is a great opportunity for you to display your problem-solving skills, as well as your resourceful nature and leadership skills.

17: How do you perform in a job with clearly-defined objectives and goals?
Answer:

It is important to consider the position when answering this question – clearly, it is best if you can excel in a job with clearly-defined objectives and goals (particularly if you're in an entry level or sales position). However, if you're applying for a position with a leadership role or creative aspect to it, be sure to focus on the ways that you additionally enjoy the challenges of developing and implementing your own ideas.

18: How do you perform in a job where you have great decision-making power?
Answer:
The interviewer wants to know that, if hired, you won't be the type of employee who needs constant supervision or who asks for advice, authority, or feedback every step of the way. Explain that you work well in a decisive, productive environment, and that you look forward to taking initiative in your position.

19: If you saw another employee doing something dishonest or unethical, what would you do?
Answer:
In the case of witnessing another employee doing something dishonest, it is always best to act in accordance with company policies for such a situation – and if you don't know what this company's specific policies are, feel free to simply state that you would handle it according to the policy and by reporting it to the appropriate persons in charge. If you are aware of the company's policies (such as if you are seeking a promotion within your own company), it is best to specifically outline your actions according to the policy.

20: Tell me about a time when you learned something on your own that later helped in your professional life.
Answer:
This question is important because it allows the interviewer to gain insight into your dedication to learning and advancement. Choose an example solely from your personal life, and provide a

brief anecdote ending in the lesson you learned. Then, explain in a clear and thorough manner how this lesson has translated into a usable skill or practice in your position.

21: Tell me about a time when you developed a project idea at work.

Answer:

Choose a project idea that you developed that was typical of projects you might complete in the new position. Outline where your idea came from, the type of research you did to ensure its success and relevancy, steps that were included in the project, and the end results. Offer specific before and after statistics, to show its success.

22: Tell me about a time when you took a risk on a project.

Answer:

Whether the risk involved something as complex as taking on a major project with limited resources or time, or simply volunteering for a task that was outside your field of experience, show that you are willing to stretch out of your comfort zone and to try new things. Offer specific examples of why something you did was risky, and explain what you learned in the process – or how this prepared you for a job objective you later faced in your career.

23: What would you tell someone who was looking to get into this field?

Answer:

This question allows you to be the expert – and will show the interviewer that you have the knowledge and experience to go along with any training and education on your resume. Offer your knowledge as advice of unexpected things that someone entering the field may encounter, and be sure to end with positive advice such as the passion or dedication to the work that is required to truly succeed.

24: Why did you choose your college major?

Answer:

It's important to display interest in your work, and if your major is related to your current field, it will be simple for you to relate the two. Perhaps you even knew while in college that you wanted to do a job similar to this position, and so you chose the major so as to receive the education and training you needed to succeed. If your major doesn't relate clearly, it's still important to express a sense of passion for your choice, and to specify the importance of pursuing something that matters to you – which is how you made the decision to come to your current career field instead.

25: Tell me about your college experience.

Answer:

It's best to keep this answer positive – don't focus on parties, pizza, or procrastinating. Instead, offer a general summary of the benefits you received in college, followed by an anecdote of a favorite professor or course that opened up your way of thinking about the field you're in. This is a great opportunity for you to show your passion for your career, make sure to answer enthusiastically and confidently.

26: What is the most unique thing about yourself that you would bring to this position?

Answer:

This question is often asked as a close to an interview, and it gives you a final chance to highlight your best qualities to the employer. Treat the question like a sort of review, and explain why your specific mix of education, experience, and passions will be the ideal combination for the employer. Remain confident but humble, and keep your answer to about two minutes.

27: How did your last job stand up to your previous expectations of it?

Answer:

While it's okay to discuss what you learned if you expected too much out of a previous job, it's best to keep this question away from negative statements or portrayals. Focus your answer around what your previous job did hold that you had expected, and how much you enjoyed those aspects of the position.

28: How did you become interested in this field?
Answer:
This is the chance for you to show your passion for your career – and the interviewer will be assured that you are a great candidate if it's obvious that you enjoy your job. You can include a brief anecdote here in order to make your interest personal, but be sure that it is *brief*. Offer specific names of mentors or professors who aided in your discovery, and make it clear that you love what you do.

29: What was the greatest thing you learned while in school?
Answer:
By offering a lesson you learned outside of the classroom, you can show the interviewer your capacity for creativity, learning, and reflection. The practical lessons you learned in the classroom are certainly invaluable in their own right and may pertain closely to the position, but showing the mastery of a concept that you had to learn on your own will highlight your growth potential.

30: Tell me about a time when you had to learn a different skill set for a new position.
Answer:
Use a specific example to describe what you had to learn and how you set about outlining goals and tasks for yourself. It's important to show that you mastered the skill largely from your dedication to learning it, and because of the systematic approach you took to developing and honing your individual education. Additionally, draw connections between the skill you learned and the new position, and show how well prepared you are for the job.

31: Tell me about a person who has been a great influence in your career.

Answer:

It's important to make this answer easy to relate to – your story should remind the interviewer of the person who was most influential in his or her own career. Explain what you learned from this person and why they inspired you, and how you hope to model them later in your career with future successes.

32: What would this person tell me about you?

Answer:

Most importantly, if this person is one of your references – they had better know who you are! There are all too many horror stories of professors or past employers being called for a reference, and not being able to recall when they knew you or why you were remarkable, which doesn't send a very positive message to potential employers. This person should remember you as being enthusiastic, passionate, and motivated to learn and succeed.

33: What is the most productive time of day for you?

Answer:

This is a trick question – you should be equally productive all day! While it's normal to become extra motivated for certain projects, and also true that some tasks will require additional work, be sure to emphasize to the interviewer that working diligently throughout the entirety of the day comes naturally to you.

34: What was the most responsibility you were given at your previous job?

Answer:

This question provides you with an opportunity to elaborate on responsibilities that may or may not be on your resume. For instance, your resume may not have allowed room to discuss individual projects you worked on that were really outside the scope of your job responsibilities, but you can tell the interviewer here about the additional work you did and how it translated into new skills and a richer career experience for you.

35: Do you believe you were compensated fairly at your last job?
Answer:
Remember to stay positive, and to avoid making negative comments about your previous employer. If you were not compensated fairly, simply state that you believe your qualities and experience were outside the compensation limitations of the old job, and that you're looking forward to an opportunity that is more in line with the place you're at in your career.

36: Tell me about a time when you received feedback on your work, and enacted it.
Answer:
Try to give an example of feedback your received early in your career, and the steps you took to incorporate it with your work. The most important part of this question is to display the way you learned from the feedback, as well as your willingness to accept suggestions from your superiors. Be sure to offer reflection and understanding of how the feedback helped your work to improve.

37: Tell me about a time when you received feedback on your work that you did not agree with, or thought was unfair. How did you handle it?
Answer:
When explaining that you did not agree with particular feedback or felt it was unfair, you'll need to justify tactfully why the feedback was inaccurate. Then, explain how you communicated directly with the person who offered the feedback, and, most importantly, how you listened to their response, analyzed it, and then came to a mutual agreement.

38: What was your favorite job, and why?
Answer:
It's best if your favorite job relates to the position you're currently applying for, as you can then easily draw connections between

why you enjoyed that job and why you are interested in the current position. Additionally, it is extremely important to explain why you've qualified the particular job as your favorite, and what aspects of it you would look for in another job, so that the interviewer can determine whether or not you are a good fit.

39: Tell me about an opportunity that your last position did not allow you to achieve.
Answer:
Stay focused on the positive, and be understanding of the limitations of your previous position. Give a specific example of a goal or career objective that you were not able to achieve, but rather than expressing disappointment over the missed opportunity, discuss the ways you're looking forward to the chance to grow in a new position.

40: Tell me about the worst boss you ever had.
Answer:
It's important to keep this answer brief, and positively focused. While you may offer a couple of short, critical assessments of your boss, focus on the things you learned from working with such an individual, and remain sympathetic to challenges the boss may have faced.

41: Describe a time when you communicated a difficult or complicated idea to a coworker.
Answer:
Start by explaining the idea briefly to the interviewer, and then give an overview of why it was necessary to break it down further to the coworker. Finally, explain the idea in succinct steps, so the interviewer can see your communication abilities and skill in simplification.

42: What situations do you find it difficult to communicate in?
Answer:
Even great communicators will often find particular situations

that are more difficult to communicate effectively in, so don't be afraid to answer this question honestly. Be sure to explain why the particular situation you name is difficult for you, and try to choose an uncommon answer such as language barrier or in time of hardship, rather than a situation such as speaking to someone of higher authority.

43: What are the key components of good communication?
Answer:
Some of the components of good communication include an environment that is free from distractions, feedback from the listener, and revision or clarification from the speaker when necessary. Refer to basic communication models where necessary, and offer to go through a role-play sample with the interviewer in order to show your skills.

44: Tell me about a time when you solved a problem through communication?
Answer:
Solving problems through communication is key in the business world, so choose a specific situation from your previous job in which you navigated a messy situation by communicating effectively through the conflict. Explain the basis of the situation, as well as the communication steps you took, and end with a discussion of why communicating through the problem was so important to its resolution.

45: Tell me about a time when you had a dispute with another employee. How did you resolve the situation?
Answer:
Make sure to use a specific instance, and explain step-by-step the scenario, what you did to handle it, and how it was finally resolved. The middle step, how you handled the dispute, is clearly the most definitive – describe the types of communication you used, and how you used compromise to reach a decision. Conflict resolution is an important skill for any employee to have, and is

one that interviewers will search for to determine both how likely you are to be involved in disputes, and how likely they are to be forced to become involved in the dispute if one arises.

46: Do you build relationships quickly with people, or take more time to get to know them?

Answer:
Either of these options can display good qualities, so determine which style is more applicable to you. Emphasize the steps you take in relationship-building over the particular style, and summarize briefly why this works best for you.

47: Describe a time when you had to work through office politics to solve a problem.

Answer:
Try to focus on the positives in this question, so that you can use the situation to your advantage. Don't portray your previous employer negatively, and instead use a minimal instance (such as paperwork or a single individual), to highlight how you worked through a specific instance resourcefully. Give examples of communication skills or problem-solving you used in order to achieve a resolution.

48: Tell me about a time when you persuaded others to take on a difficult task?

Answer:
This question is an opportunity to highlight both your leadership and communication skills. While the specific situation itself is important to offer as background, focus on how you were able to persuade the others, and what tactics worked the best.

49: Tell me about a time when you successfully persuaded a group to accept your proposal.

Answer:
This question is designed to determine your resourcefulness and your communication skills. Explain the ways in which you took

into account different perspectives within the group, and created a presentation that would be appealing and convincing to all members. Additionally, you can pump up the proposal itself by offering details about it that show how well-executed it was.

50: Tell me about a time when you had a problem with another person, that, in hindsight, you wished you had handled differently.

Answer:

The key to this question is to show your capabilities of reflection and your learning process. Explain the situation, how you handled it at the time, what the outcome of the situation was, and finally, how you would handle it now. Most importantly, tell the interviewer why you would handle it differently now – did your previous solution create stress on the relationship with the other person, or do you wish that you had stood up more for what you wanted? While you shouldn't elaborate on how poorly you handled the situation before, the most important thing is to show that you've grown and reached a deeper level of understanding as a result of the conflict.

51: Tell me about a time when you negotiated a conflict between other employees.

Answer:

An especially important question for those interviewing for a supervisory role – begin with a specific situation, and explain how you communicated effectively to each individual. For example, did you introduce a compromise? Did you make an executive decision? Or, did you perform as a mediator and encourage the employees to reach a conclusion on their own?

INDEX

26: How many types of pop-up boxes does JavaScript have? What are those?

27: Does creating an alert box prompt the user to respond with OK or Cancel?

28: What are functions in JavaScript and where are they placed?

Values, Arrays and Operators

29: What does the keyword null mean in JavaScript?

30: What does the value undefined mean in JavaScript?

31: Do the null and undefined values have the same conversion in Boolean, numeric and string context?

32: What are Boolean values?

33: Can a Boolean value be converted into numeric context?

34: What happens when a number is dropped where a Boolean value is expected to be?

35: What are objects in JavaScript?

36: What is an array in JavaScript?

37: From which version forward has JavaScript stopped using ASCII character set?

38: What is the scope of a variable in JavaScript?

39: In the body of the code which variable with the same name has more importance over the other: the local or the global variable?

40: How many types of undefined variables can we find in JavaScript?

41: What are the (=) (===) and what do they do in JavaScript?

42: How many types of operators can we find in JavaScript?

43: How many types of comparison operators does JavaScript contain?

44: Can comparison be done on any type of operands?

45: What are logical operators and how are they used in JavaScript?

46: Does JavaScript contain classes?

47: What is an object in JavaScript?

48: How are classes and objects in JavaScript named and why?

49: What are class properties in JavaScript?

50: What are class methods in JavaScript?

51: Do class properties and class methods have a global and local range?

52: How do JavaScript equality operators compare objects?

53: Are the null and undefined values for the variable same?

54: What is the difference between "===" and "=="?

55: What is the function of delete operator in JavaScript?

56: How will you clip the particular portion of an element?

Modules, Characters and Attributes

57: How is a module in JavaScript written so that it can be used by any script or module?

58: How are regular expressions represented and created in JavaScript?

59: How do you combine literal characters in JavaScript?

60: What document properties does a document contain?

61: How many types of DOM document object collections can we find in JavaScript?

62: Does use of DOM properties allow you to change the structure of a document?

63: How are document objects named in JavaScript?

Event Handlers and DOM

64: How are event handlers defined in JavaScript?

65: What do the HTMLInputElement and HTMLFormElementinterfaces define in HTML DOM?

66: How many levels of DOM standard are currently released?

67: Are there any more levels of DOM?

68: What does the Node interface define in DOM?

69: How do you find document elements in a HTML document?

70: How are documents created and modified in DOM?

71: How can you build a DOM tree of arbitrary document content?

72: How do you find document elements in IE4?

73: How to access Html attributes using DOM?

74: What is the difference between getAttribute() and getAttributeNode()?

75: What are the event handlers in JavaScript?

76: Can you use two or more functions in onclick event?

Keywords, CSS and CSS2

77: What is the "this" keyword in JavaScript?

78: What does lexically scoped in JavaScript mean?

79: Is the following expression correct: element.style.font-family= "arial";?

Statements and Functions

80: How can you replace an if-else statement in JavaScript?

81: What is a "memoization" method in JavaScript?

82: What does 2+3+"1" evaluate to?

Roles of JavaScript, Scripts and Events

83: Give some examples of the role that JavaScript has on the Web.

84: Give an example on how JavaScript can be used in URLs.

85: How are scripts in JavaScript executed?

86: What do scripts placed in the <head> part of an HTML document do?

87: What do scripts placed in the <body> part of an HTML document do?

88: When does the browser fire an onload event?

89: When does the onunload event trigger and what does it do?

90: What about reading, writing a file? How can we do this in JavaScript?

91: What is "cross-site scripting"?

92: What are JavaScript timers? Give examples and explain one of them.

93: What is the "History" object?

94: What is the "Screen" object?

95: What is the "Navigator" object?

96: What is "onreset" in JavaScript?

97: What is void 0 in JavaScript?

98: What is the best practice to place the JavaScript codes?

99: How to prevent caching of web pages in temporary internet files folder?

100: Why adding of meta tag in first header will not prevent caching of the Web page?

101: What is the purpose of meta tag?

102: How will you resolve looping problem in JavaScript?

103: Give any example for resolving looping problem.

104: When is the Execution context created and what are the primary components?

105: When is the Execution context stack created?

106: How is the outer scope environment references maintained?

107: How will you read or write in a file using JavaScript?

108: How will you create rich, responsive display and editor user interface?

109: Which is the new JavaScript engine developed for internet explorer9 by Microsoft?

110: What is Node.js?

111: Which is alternative to XML for data exchange in JavaScript?

112: What are the sub-components of dynamic component in JavaScript?

Opening and Manipulating Windows

113: How can you open a new window using JavaScript?

114: How can you close a window using JavaScript?

115: What does the "location" function do in JavaScript?

116: What other properties besides Href can we find in the "location" function in JavaScript?

117: What happens when a string value is added to the location function in JavaScript?

118: What is the history object in JavaScript?

119: Which are the methods supported by the history object in JavaScript?

120: How many and which are the coordinates of a browser within the HTML document?

Objects and their Properties in JavaScript

121: What is the screen object in JavaScript?

122: What is the Navigator object in JavaScript?

123: Name the properties of Navigator in JavaScript.

124: What happens when confirm() or prompt() methods are used in JavaScript?

125: What happens when the mouse is moved over a hyperlink in JavaScript?

126: What does the "defaultStatus" property do in JavaScript?

127: What is the "onerror" property in JavaScript?

128: What arguments does the error handler receive when an error occurs in JavaScript?

129: In addition to the three arguments that the error handler receives, is its return value of any importance?

130: How can JavaScript code can refer to a window or frame object?

131: What is a DOM (Document Object Model)?

132: What does the method write() of the Document object do?

133: How will you determine an object type?

134: What is alert and confirm box in java script?

135: What are the properties of array object?

136: What are the sub objects of the windows object in JavaScript?

137: What is the use of userAgent of navigator object?

138: What are the ways to delete the property of an object and how?

139: What is the use of eval() in JSON?

140: What are the advantages of JSON over XML?

141: How can the properties of JavaScript objects be accessed?

142: What are the objects of navigator objects?

143: How to access the properties of the main window from secondary window?

144: How will you load the previous and next url from the history list?

145: How will you determine whether the browser has cookies enabled?

JavaScript and HTML

146: How can you change the font size of an Element in JavaScript? Give an example.

147: How can you submit a form using JavaScript?

148: How can you set the background color of an HMTL document?

149: Name the Boolean operators in JavaScript.

150: How can we determine the state of a checkbox in JavaScript?

151: How can you create an HTML button and what is the event called when the button is pressed?

152: How will you make loading of JavaScript code after Html by the browser?

153: Which popup allows the user to enter the input?

154: What are the ways to display the message on screen?

155: How will you reload the page from server using JavaScript?

156: How will you display large tables effectively in JavaScript?

157: How will you create pop window using JavaScript?

158: How will you fix the errors that make the JavaScript engines difficult to perform optimization?

159: How will you make secure JavaScript code?

160: How will you add the external JavaScript file?

161: Is it possible to break up a string in a JavaScript code?

162: What is the use of "wait" property in cursor style?

163: What are the properties that can be set in the background properties?

164: What are the ways to set the background color?

165: How will you add JavaScript files dynamically?

166: How will you get the current "x and y" co-ordinate value of the window when it is scrolled?

167: What are the methods to create remote window?

168: How will you get the height of the browser window?

169: How will you get the language code of the linked page?

170: How would you input a file?

JavaScript Forms

171: What is the importance of the "name" attribute of a <form> tag?

172: What are the event handlers of the form element?

173: What does "onchange" event handler do?

174: What is a "cookie"?

175: What does the "new" operator do?

176: What does <optgroup> tag do in JavaScript?

177: Comparison between session state and view state.

178: Which function is best for fast execution: window.onload or onDocumentReady?

179: What is the purpose of "visibility" property in JavaScript?

180: What are the ways to make an element visible/hidden?

181: How will you disable the html form fields, for instance password field?

182: How will you select the contents in the text field, say password?

183: How will you display the id of the form and the name attribute of the hidden element?

184: How will you get the last row from a table in JavaScript?

185: How will you create and delete caption to a table?

186: How will you create a text area and make it read-only?

187: How will you change the caption display position of a table?

JavaScript Constructors

188: What does a JavaScript constructor do?

189: What is the value that the constructor function returns?

190: How many types of common object methods can we find in JavaScript?

191: How does class hierarchy manifest themselves in JavaScript?

192: What does "overriding method" mean?

193: How can you create an XML document in Firefox using JavaScript?

194: How are images accessed from JavaScript?

195: Where is the arguments() array placed in JavaScript?

196: Which are the properties of the arguments object in JavaScript?

197: What happens when a function is invoked with the arguments object?

Miscellaneous Arguments, Functions and Methods in JavaScript

198: What does arguments.callee do in JavaScript?

199: What does arguments.length do in JavaScript?

200: What other JavaScript method you know that is similar with shift() method?

201: How can you remove a page from the browser history?

202: How can you pass data between pages using cookies?

203: What is the difference between resizeTo() and resizeBy() methods?

204: What's the difference between moveTo() and moveBy() methods?

205: How can a window that is buried beneath other windows be brought back to the front?

206: What happens when a string argument is passed with the Date() constructor in JavaScript?

207: Which are the arguments of the Date() constructor in JavaScript?

208: What does URIError indicate in JavaScript?

209: What does the encodeURIComponent function do in JavaScript?

210: What does the string argument do in JavaScript?

211: What is and what does the escape() function do in JavaScript?

212: What does the apply() function do in JavaScript and which are its arguments?

213: What does the getClass() function do in JavaScript?

214: What is Infinity in JavaScript?

215: What does the exec() method do in JavaScript?

216: What happens when the exec() method is invoked on a nonglobal pattern?

217: Does exec() include full details of every match even if regexp is not global?

218: What is an anchor in JavaScript?

219: What does the focus() method do in JavaScript?

220: Is JSObject a JavaScript object?

221: What does the call() method of JSObject class do?

222: What does the eval() method of the JSObject do?

223: What does the getSlot() method of the JSObject do?

224: What does the removeMember() method of the JSObject do?

225: What does the setMember() method of the JSObject do?

226: What does the toString() method of JSObject do?

227: What does the (n) argument represent in isFinite(n) and what does it return?

228: What does the isNaN() function do in JavaScript?

229: What does the setYear() function do in JavaScript?

230: What does the join() method do in JavaScript?

231: How will you pop the last element from an existing array?

232: How to pop the first element from an existing array?

233: How will you add one or more elements to the end of the existing array?

234: How will you add one or more elements to the beginning of the existing array?

235: How will you reverse the elements in an array?

236: What does the Array.slice(start,end) method do in JavaScript and how to retrieve the elements within the selected position in an array?

237: What does the Array.sort() method do in JavaScript?

238: What is encodeURI( ) and encodeURIComponent( )?

239: What is decodeURI( ) and decodeURIComponent( )?

240: What does the splice( ) function do in JavaScript?

241: How will you print the current window using JavaScript?

242: How will you get default value when an argument is not passed in calling function?

243: How will you encode and decode a string?

244: How will you pass a function as argument to another function?

245: What is the need for callback function?

246: How will you get a substring from a string in JavaScript?

247: How will you get the function (fn1) which recently called the current function (fn2)?

248: How will you execute the page that is about to be unloaded, before the execution of onload()?

249: How will you find whether the window is closed or not?

250: How will you call a function repeatedly for a particular interval of time?

251: What is the difference between test and exec function?

HR Questions

1: Would you rather receive more authority or more responsibility at work?

2: What do you do when someone in a group isn't contributing their fair share?

3: Tell me about a time when you made a decision that was outside of your authority.

4: Are you comfortable going to supervisors with disputes?

5: If you had been in charge at your last job, what would you have done differently?

6: Do you believe employers should praise or reward employees for a job well done?

7: What do you believe is the most important quality a leader can have?

8: Tell me about a time when an unforeseen problem arose. How did you handle it?

9: Can you give me an example of a time when you were able to improve X *objective* at your previous job?

10: Tell me about a time when a supervisor did not provide specific enough direction on a project.

11: Tell me about a time when you were in charge of leading a project.

12: Tell me about a suggestion you made to a former employer that was later implemented.

13: Tell me about a time when you thought of a way something in the workplace could be done more efficiently.

14: Is there a difference between leading and managing people – which is your greater strength?

15: Do you function better in a leadership role, or as a worker on a team?

16: Tell me about a time when you discovered something in the workplace that was disrupting your (or others) productivity – what did you do about it?

17: How do you perform in a job with clearly-defined objectives and goals?

18: How do you perform in a job where you have great decision-making power?

19: If you saw another employee doing something dishonest or unethical, what would you do?

20: Tell me about a time when you learned something on your own that later helped in your professional life.

21: Tell me about a time when you developed a project idea at work.

22: Tell me about a time when you took a risk on a project.

23: What would you tell someone who was looking to get into this field?

24: Why did you choose your college major?

25: Tell me about your college experience.

26: What is the most unique thing about yourself that you would bring to this position?

27: How did your last job stand up to your previous expectations of it?

28: How did you become interested in this field?

29: What was the greatest thing you learned while in school?

30: Tell me about a time when you had to learn a different skill set for a new position.

31: Tell me about a person who has been a great influence in your career.

32: What would this person tell me about you?

33: What is the most productive time of day for you?

34: What was the most responsibility you were given at your previous job?

35: Do you believe you were compensated fairly at your last job?

36: Tell me about a time when you received feedback on your work, and enacted it.

37: Tell me about a time when you received feedback on your work that you did not agree with, or thought was unfair. How did you handle it?

38: What was your favorite job, and why?

39: Tell me about an opportunity that your last position did not allow you to achieve.

40: Tell me about the worst boss you ever had.

41: Describe a time when you communicated a difficult or complicated idea to a coworker.

42: What situations do you find it difficult to communicate in?

43: What are the key components of good communication?

44: Tell me about a time when you solved a problem through communication?

45: Tell me about a time when you had a dispute with another employee. How did you resolve the situation?

46: Do you build relationships quickly with people, or take more time to get to know them?

47: Describe a time when you had to work through office politics to solve a problem.

48: Tell me about a time when you persuaded others to take on a difficult task?

50: Tell me about a time when you had a problem with another person, that, in hindsight, you wished you had handled differently.

51: Tell me about a time when you negotiated a conflict between other employees.

Some of the following titles might also be handy:

1. .NET Interview Questions You'll Most Likely Be Asked
2. 200 Interview Questions You'll Most Likely Be Asked
3. Access VBA Programming Interview Questions You'll Most Likely Be Asked
4. Adobe ColdFusion Interview Questions You'll Most Likely Be Asked
5. Advanced Excel Interview Questions You'll Most Likely Be Asked
6. Advanced JAVA Interview Questions You'll Most Likely Be Asked
7. Advanced SAS Interview Questions You'll Most Likely Be Asked
8. AJAX Interview Questions You'll Most Likely Be Asked
9. Algorithms Interview Questions You'll Most Likely Be Asked
10. Android Development Interview Questions You'll Most Likely Be Asked
11. Ant & Maven Interview Questions You'll Most Likely Be Asked
12. Apache Web Server Interview Questions You'll Most Likely Be Asked
13. Artificial Intelligence Interview Questions You'll Most Likely Be Asked
14. ASP.NET Interview Questions You'll Most Likely Be Asked
15. Automated Software Testing Interview Questions You'll Most Likely Be Asked
16. Base SAS Interview Questions You'll Most Likely Be Asked
17. BEA WebLogic Server Interview Questions You'll Most Likely Be Asked
18. C & C++ Interview Questions You'll Most Likely Be Asked
19. C# Interview Questions You'll Most Likely Be Asked
20. C++ Internals Interview Questions You'll Most Likely Be Asked
21. CCNA Interview Questions You'll Most Likely Be Asked
22. Cloud Computing Interview Questions You'll Most Likely Be Asked
23. Computer Architecture Interview Questions You'll Most Likely Be Asked
24. Computer Networks Interview Questions You'll Most Likely Be Asked
25. Core JAVA Interview Questions You'll Most Likely Be Asked
26. Data Structures & Algorithms Interview Questions You'll Most Likely Be Asked
27. Data WareHousing Interview Questions You'll Most Likely Be Asked
28. EJB 3.0 Interview Questions You'll Most Likely Be Asked
29. Entity Framework Interview Questions You'll Most Likely Be Asked
30. Fedora & RHEL Interview Questions You'll Most Likely Be Asked
31. GNU Development Interview Questions You'll Most Likely Be Asked
32. Hibernate, Spring & Struts Interview Questions You'll Most Likely Be Asked
33. HTML, XHTML and CSS Interview Questions You'll Most Likely Be Asked
34. HTML5 Interview Questions You'll Most Likely Be Asked
35. IBM WebSphere Application Server Interview Questions You'll Most Likely Be Asked
36. iOS SDK Interview Questions You'll Most Likely Be Asked
37. Java / J2EE Design Patterns Interview Questions You'll Most Likely Be Asked
38. Java / J2EE Interview Questions You'll Most Likely Be Asked
39. Java Messaging Service Interview Questions You'll Most Likely Be Asked
40. JavaScript Interview Questions You'll Most Likely Be Asked
41. JavaServer Faces Interview Questions You'll Most Likely Be Asked
42. JDBC Interview Questions You'll Most Likely Be Asked
43. jQuery Interview Questions You'll Most Likely Be Asked
44. JSP-Servlet Interview Questions You'll Most Likely Be Asked
45. JUnit Interview Questions You'll Most Likely Be Asked
46. Linux Commands Interview Questions You'll Most Likely Be Asked
47. Linux Interview Questions You'll Most Likely Be Asked
48. Linux System Administrator Interview Questions You'll Most Likely Be Asked
49. Mac OS X Lion Interview Questions You'll Most Likely Be Asked
50. Mac OS X Snow Leopard Interview Questions You'll Most Likely Be Asked
51. Microsoft Access Interview Questions You'll Most Likely Be Asked

52. Microsoft Excel Interview Questions You'll Most Likely Be Asked
53. Microsoft Powerpoint Interview Questions You'll Most Likely Be Asked
54. Microsoft Word Interview Questions You'll Most Likely Be Asked
55. MySQL Interview Questions You'll Most Likely Be Asked
56. NetSuite Interview Questions You'll Most Likely Be Asked
57. Networking Interview Questions You'll Most Likely Be Asked
58. OOPS Interview Questions You'll Most Likely Be Asked
59. Operating Systems Interview Questions You'll Most Likely Be Asked
60. Oracle DBA Interview Questions You'll Most Likely Be Asked
61. Oracle E-Business Suite Interview Questions You'll Most Likely Be Asked
62. ORACLE PL/SQL Interview Questions You'll Most Likely Be Asked
63. Perl Interview Questions You'll Most Likely Be Asked
64. PHP Interview Questions You'll Most Likely Be Asked
65. PMP Interview Questions You'll Most Likely Be Asked
66. Python Interview Questions You'll Most Likely Be Asked
67. RESTful JAVA Web Services Interview Questions You'll Most Likely Be Asked
68. Ruby Interview Questions You'll Most Likely Be Asked
69. Ruby on Rails Interview Questions You'll Most Likely Be Asked
70. SAP ABAP Interview Questions You'll Most Likely Be Asked
71. SAS STAT and Programming Interview Questions You'll Most Likely Be Asked
72. Selenium Testing Tools Interview Questions You'll Most Likely Be Asked
73. Silverlight Interview Questions You'll Most Likely Be Asked
74. Software Repositories Interview Questions You'll Most Likely Be Asked
75. Software Testing Interview Questions You'll Most Likely Be Asked
76. SQL Server Interview Questions You'll Most Likely Be Asked
77. Tomcat Interview Questions You'll Most Likely Be Asked
78. UML Interview Questions You'll Most Likely Be Asked
79. Unix Interview Questions You'll Most Likely Be Asked
80. UNIX Shell Programming Interview Questions You'll Most Likely Be Asked
81. VB.NET Interview Questions You'll Most Likely Be Asked
82. XLXP, XSLT, XPATH, XFORMS & XQuery Interview Questions Y ou'll Most Likely Be Asked
83. XML Interview Questions You'll Most Likely Be Asked

For complete list visit

www.vibrantpublishers.com